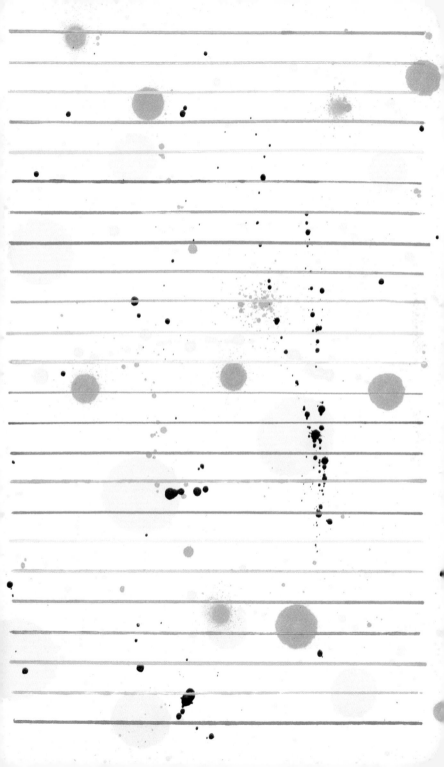

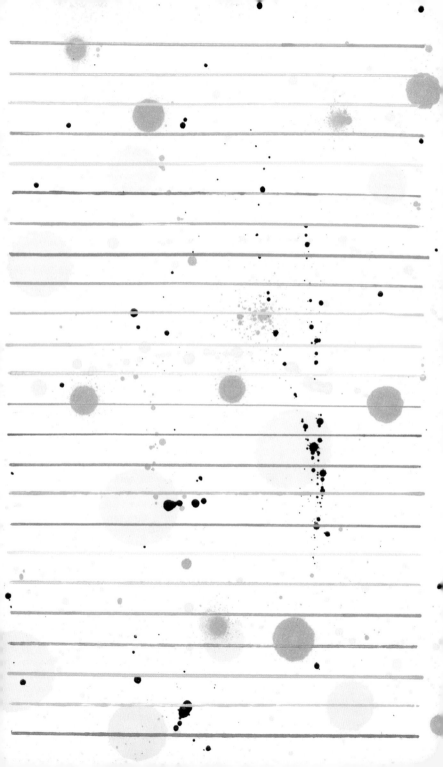

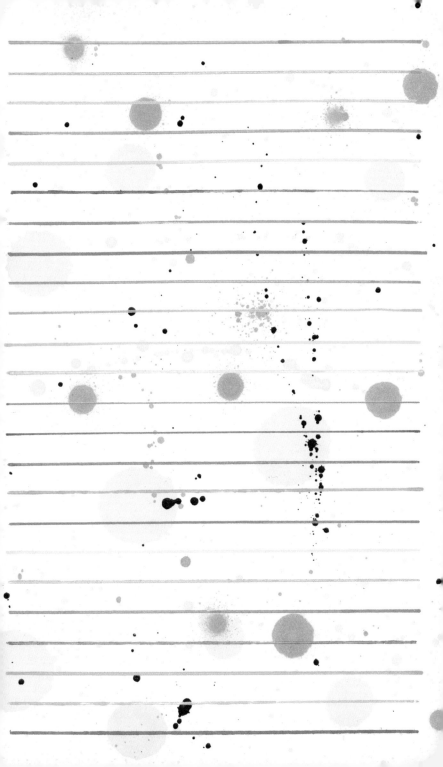

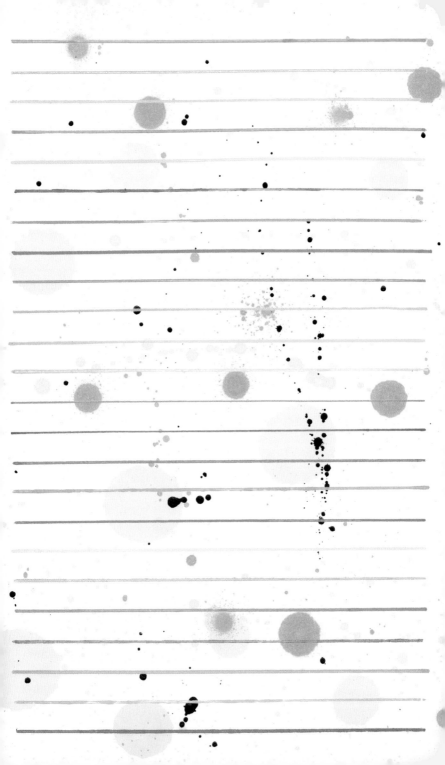

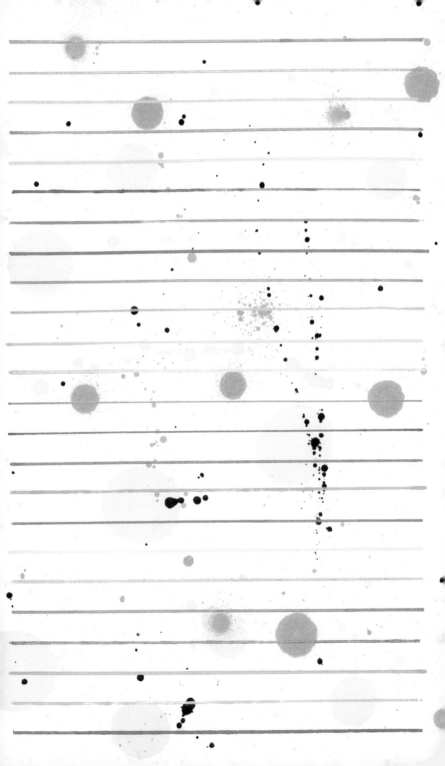

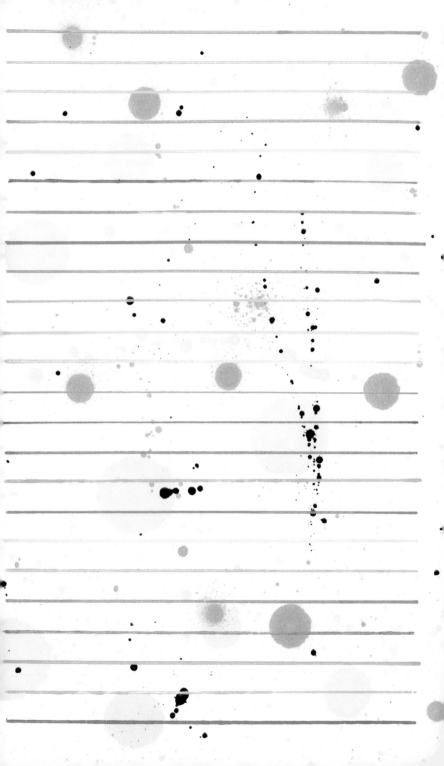

I believe all women
know in their

HEART
OF
HEARTS

that they truly are

DIVINE
and MAGICAL,
even if they've temporarily
forgotten

- Kelly Cutrone

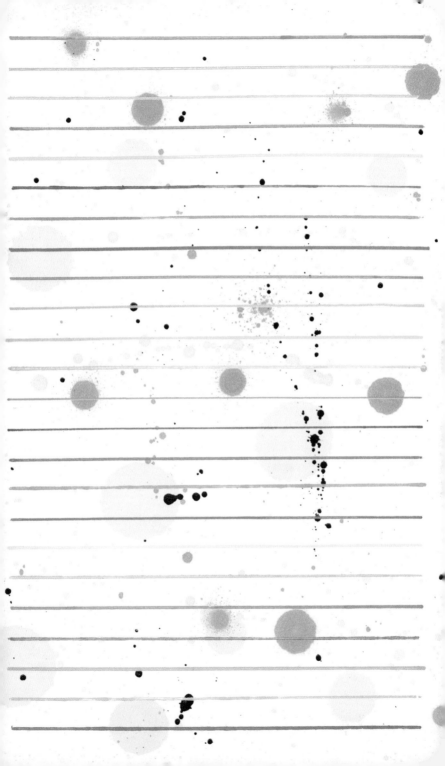

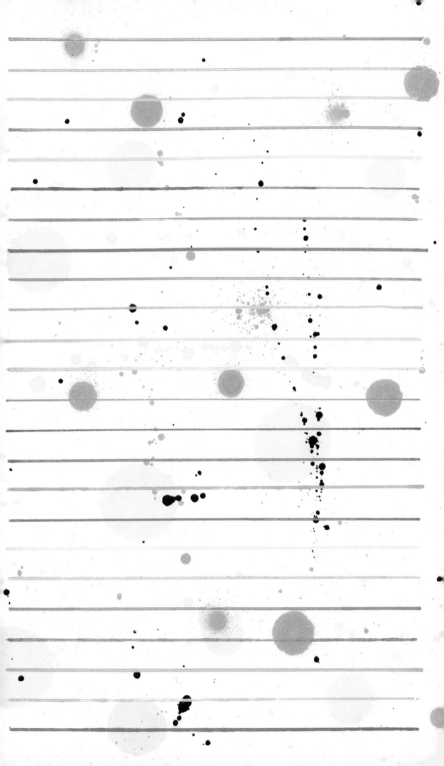

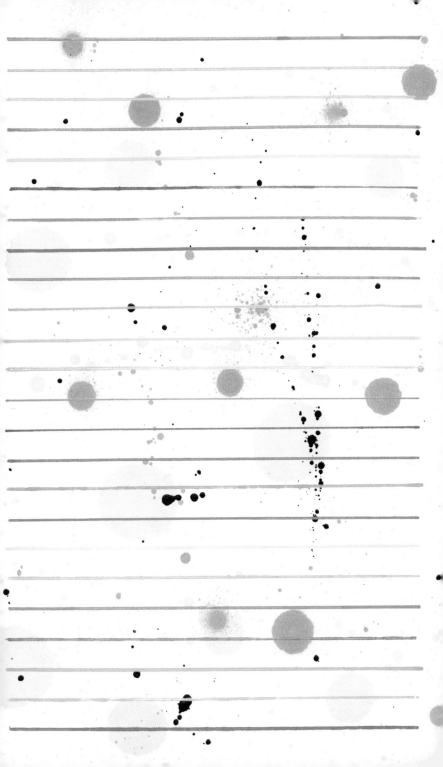

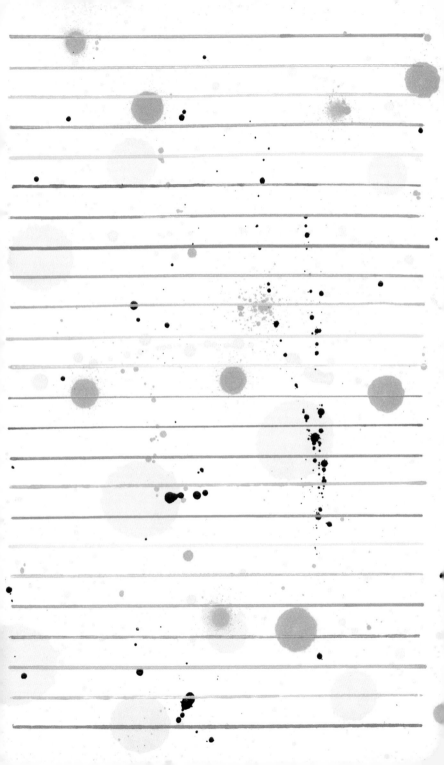

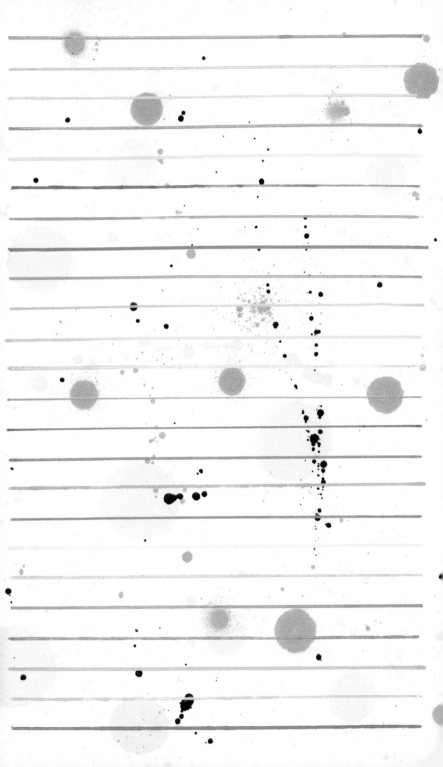

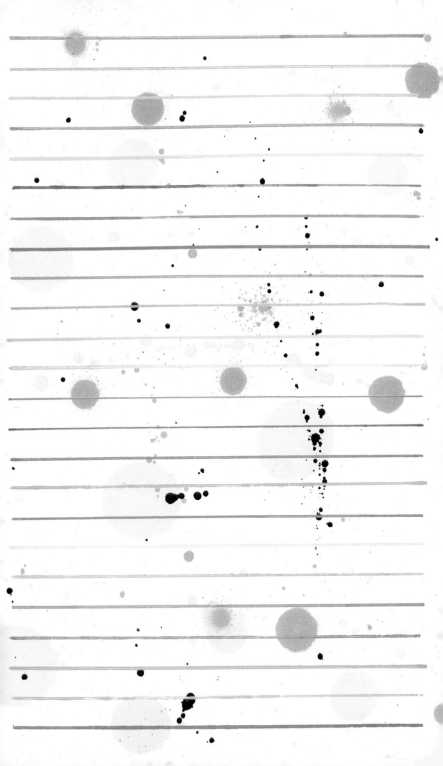

Beauty appears when something is completely and absolutely and openly itself.

-deena metzger

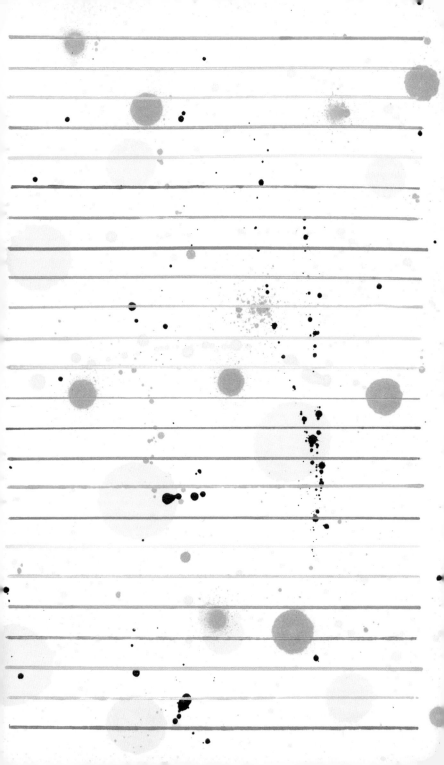

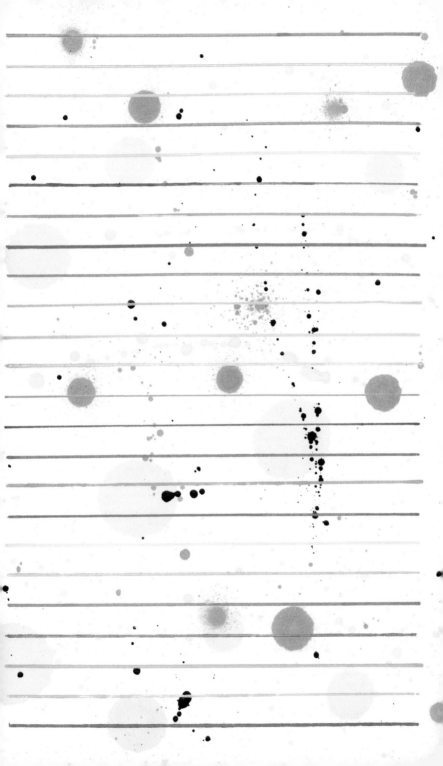

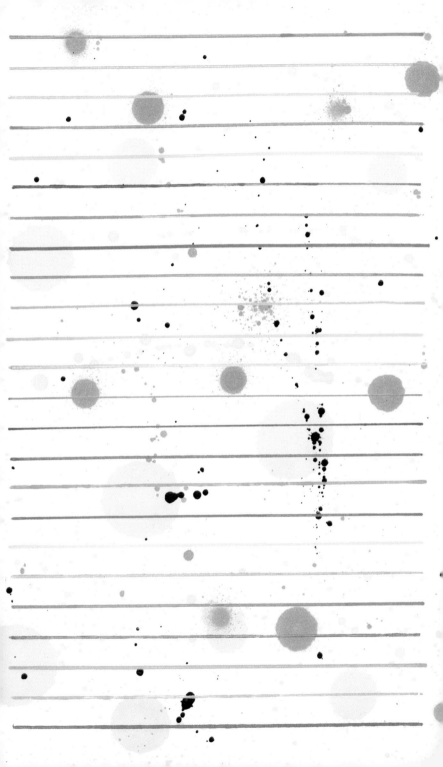

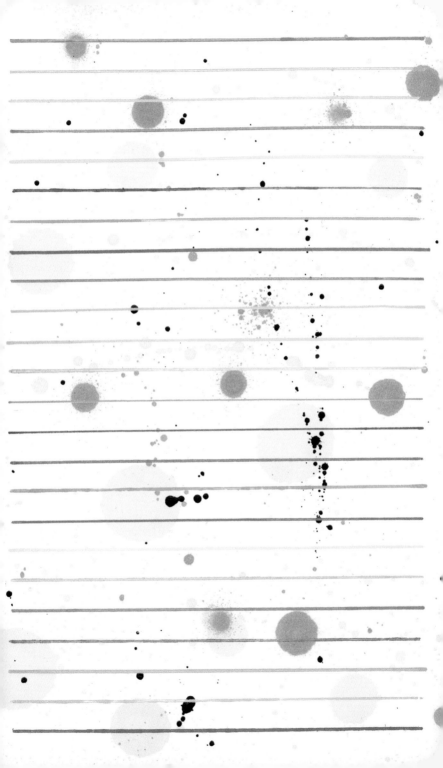

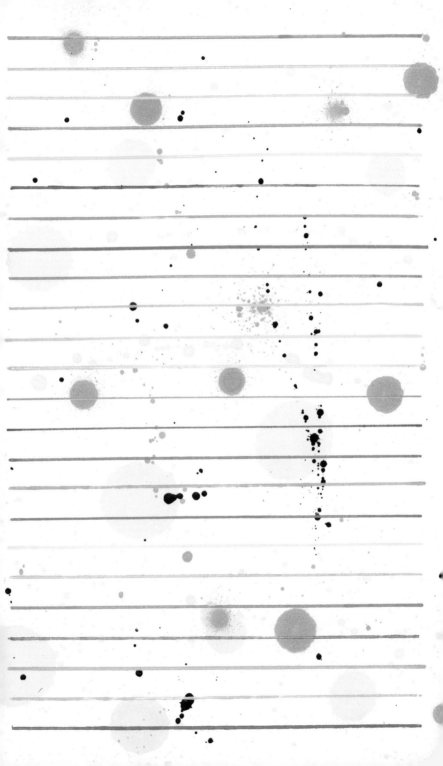

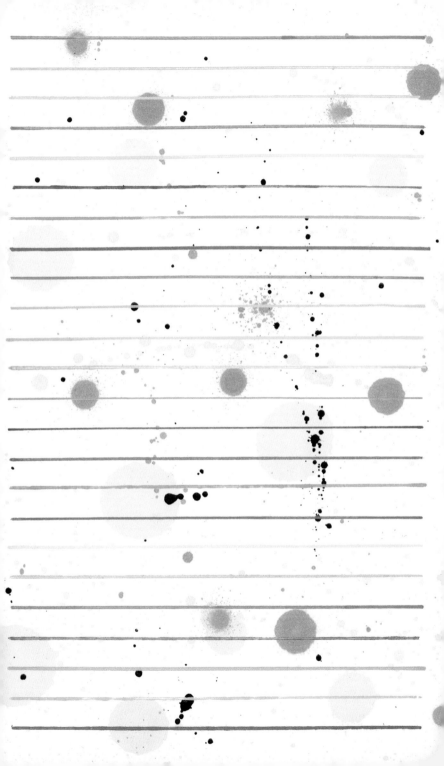

Be yourself.
Be True
to that,
to your
HEART.
- Nora Roberts

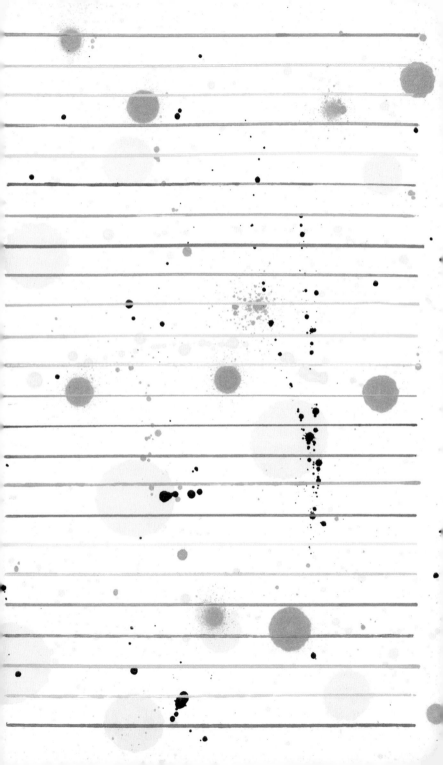

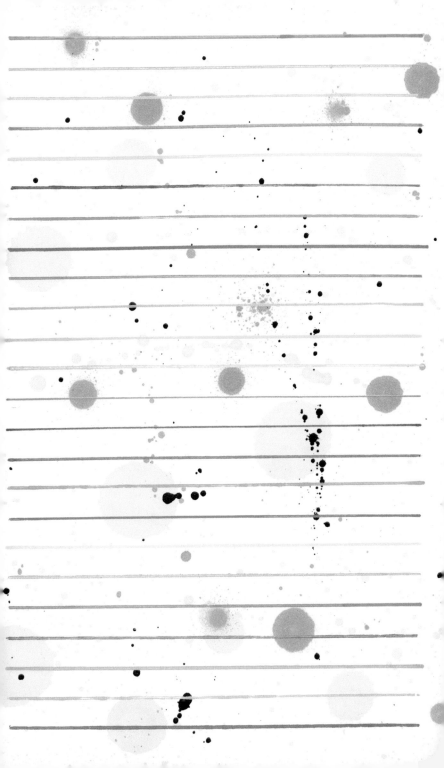

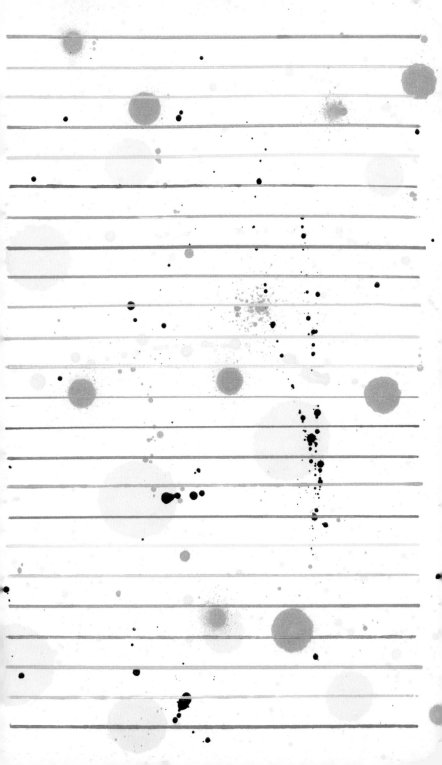

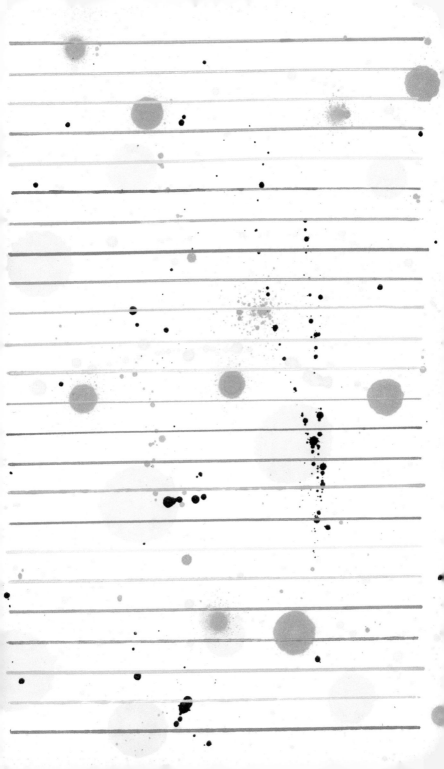

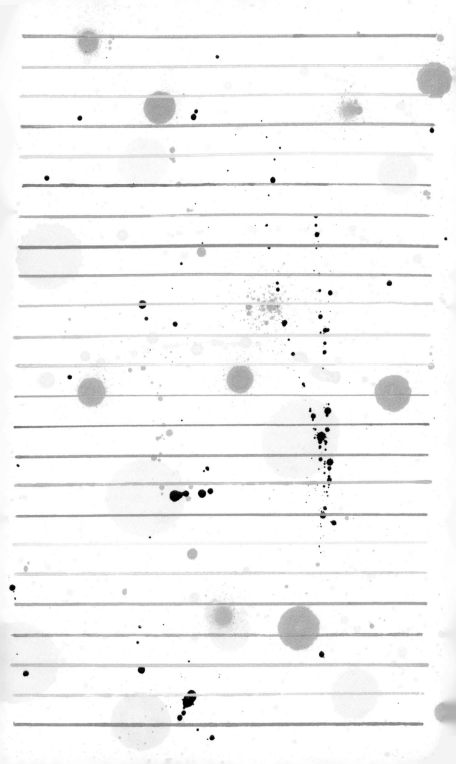

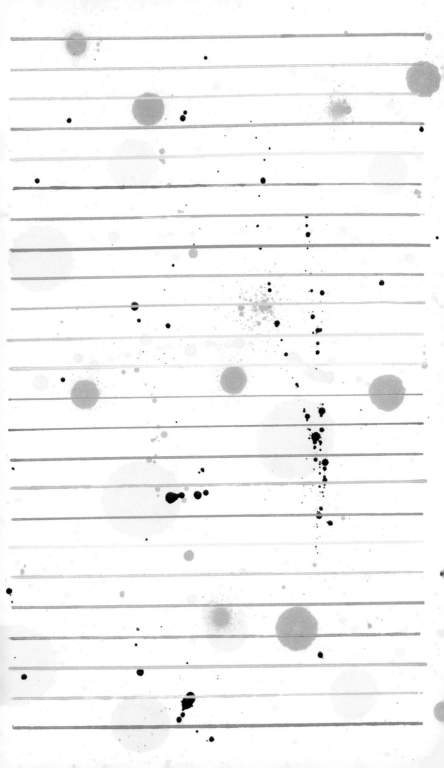

THE MOST BEAUTIFUL PEOPLE
WE HAVE KNOWN ARE THOSE
WHO HAVE KNOWN
DEFEAT, KNOWN
SUFFERING,
KNOWN STRUGGLE, KNOWN LOSS,
AND HAVE FOUND THEIR
WAY OUT OF THE DEPTHS.
THESE PERSONS HAVE AN
APPRECIATION,
A SENSITIVITY, AND AN
understanding
OF LIFE THAT FILLS THEM WITH
COMPASSION, gentleness,
AND A DEEP LOVING concern.
BEAUTIFUL PEOPLE DO NOT JUST HAPPEN.

-elisabeth kübler-ross

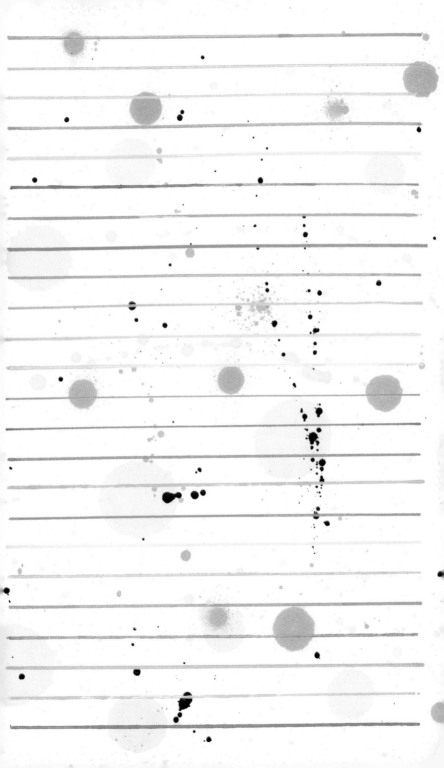

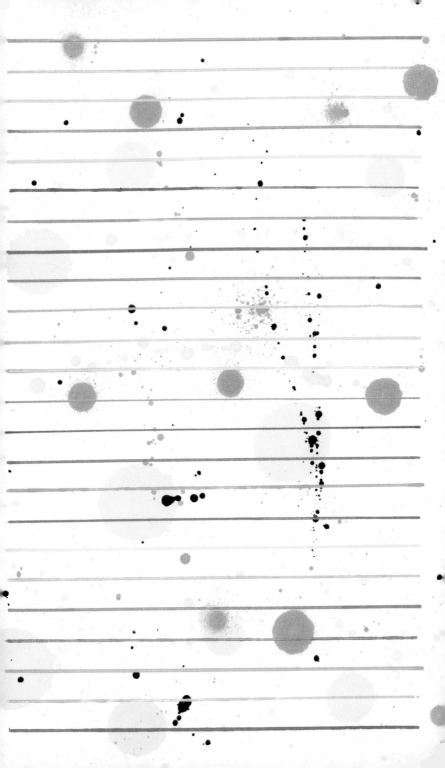

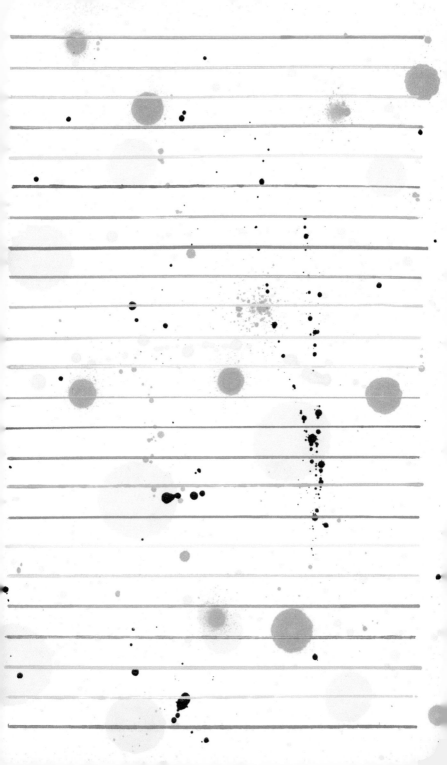

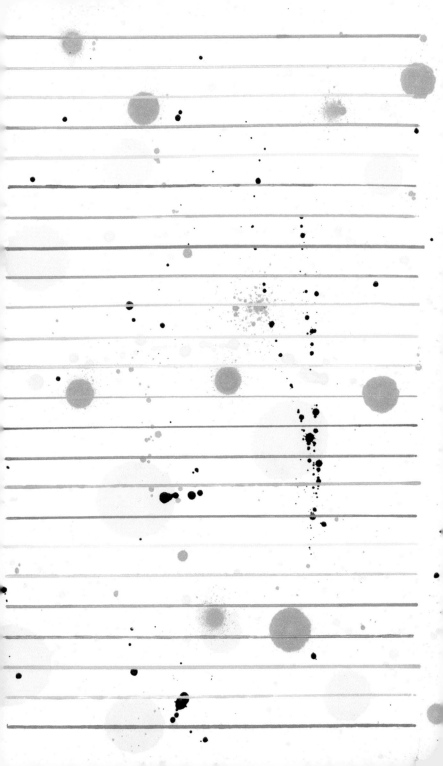

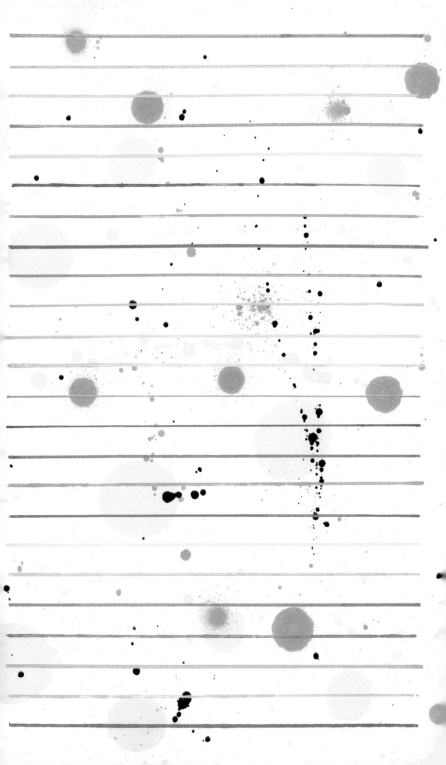

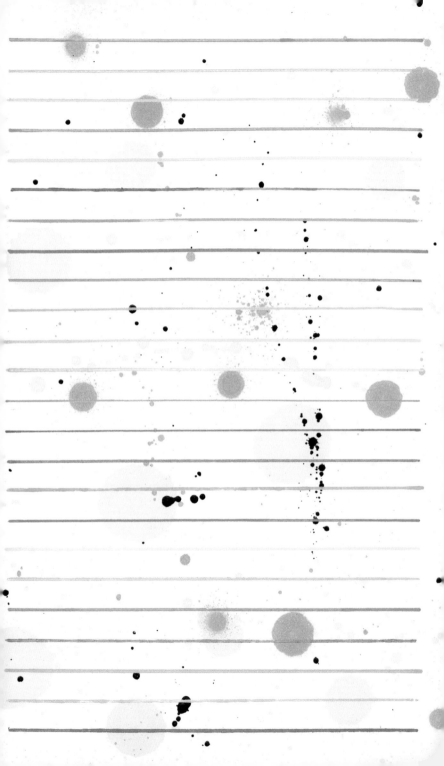

What makes you VULNERABLE makes you beautiful

-Brené Brown

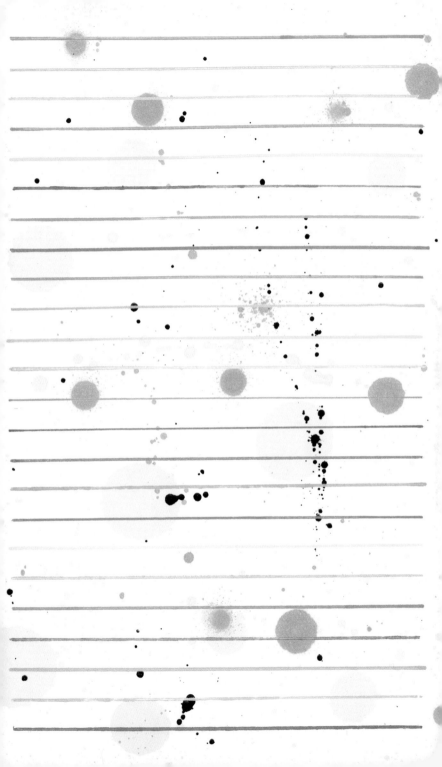

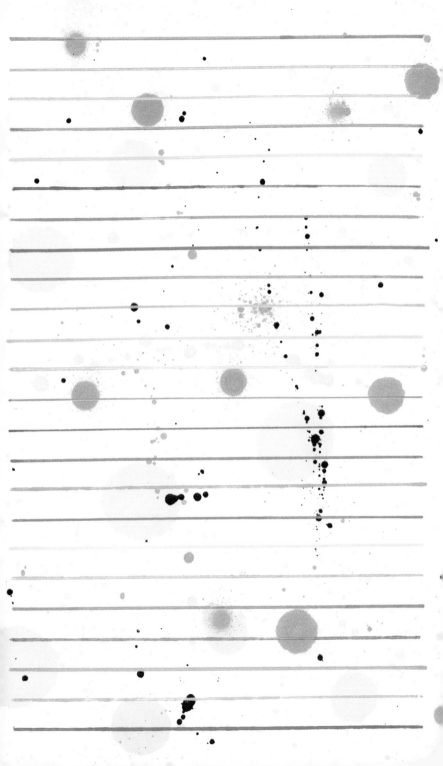

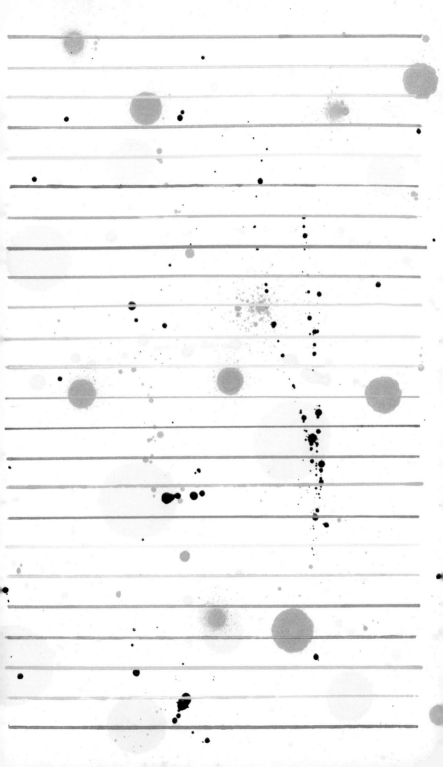

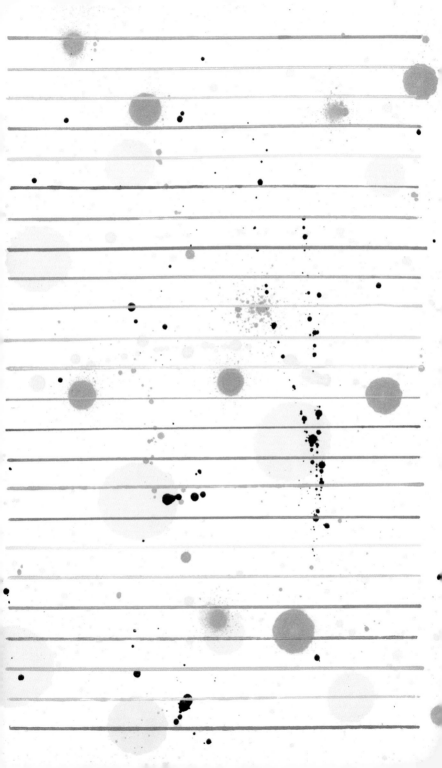

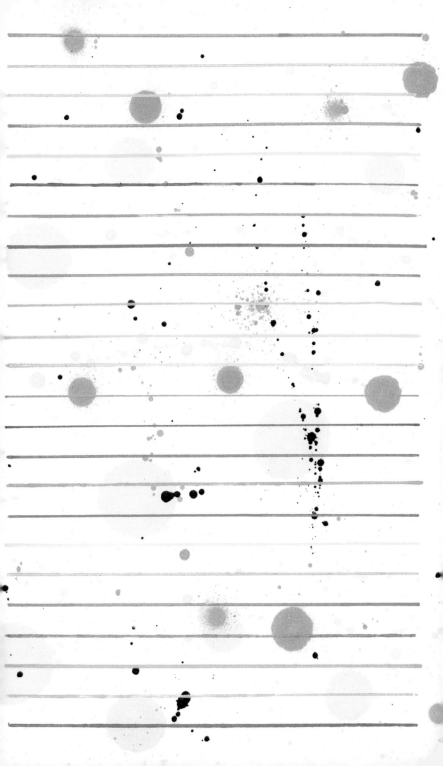

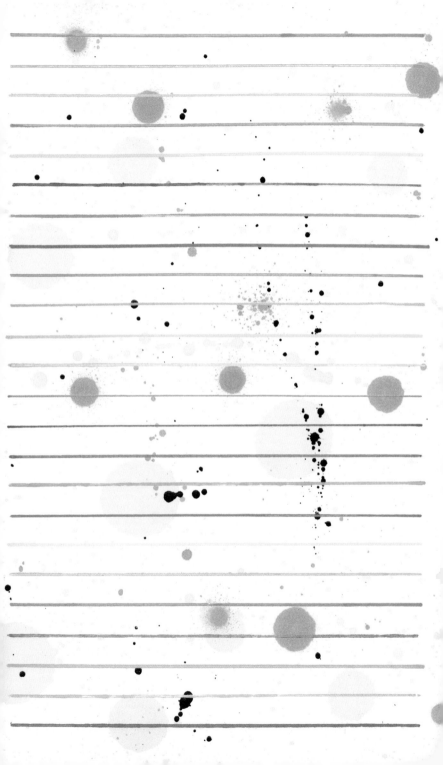

I WAS ALWAYS LOOKING outside MYSELF FOR STRENGTH AND confidence, BUT IT COMES FROM within. IT IS THERE ALL THE TIME.

-Anna Freud

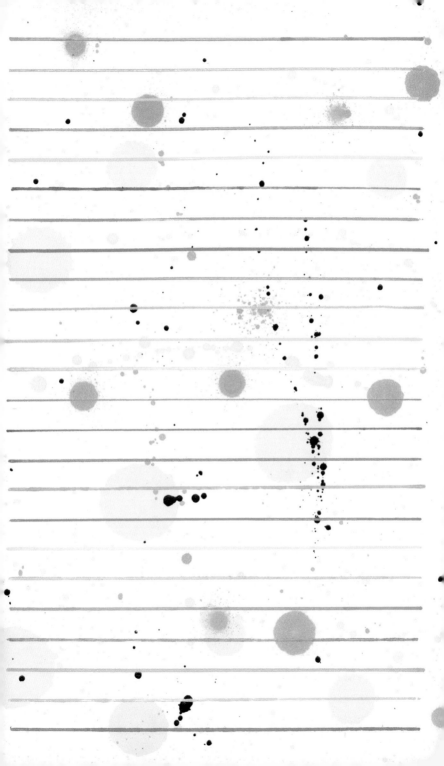

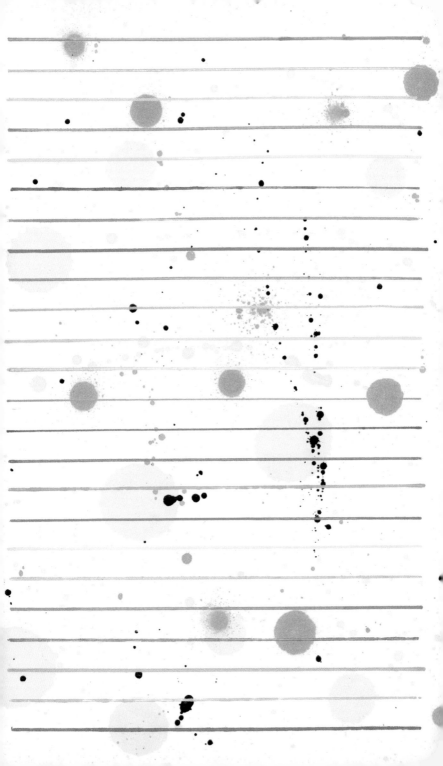

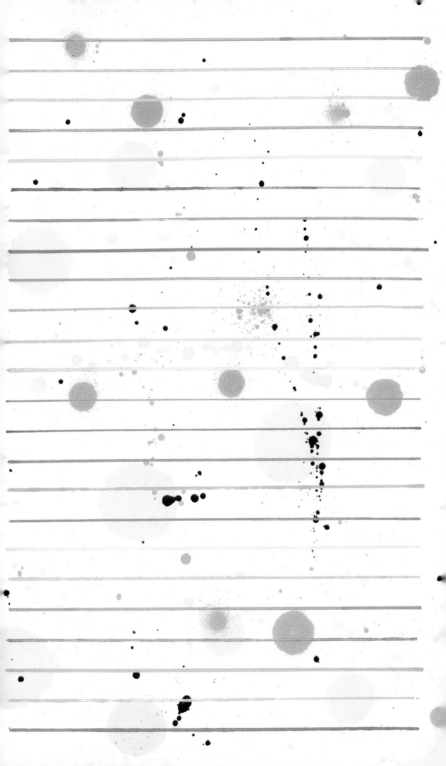

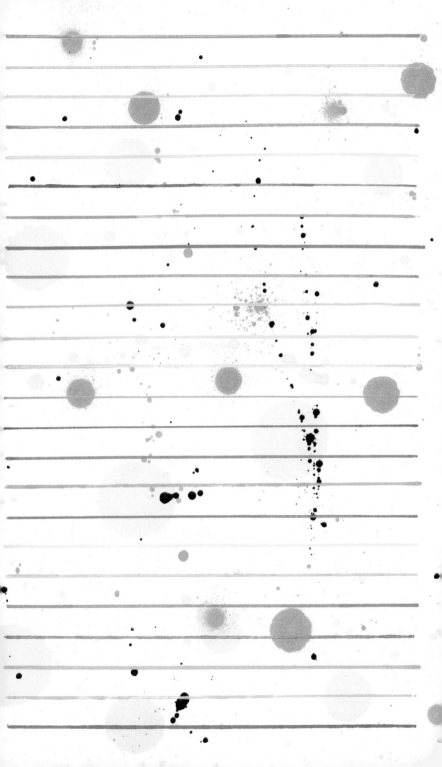

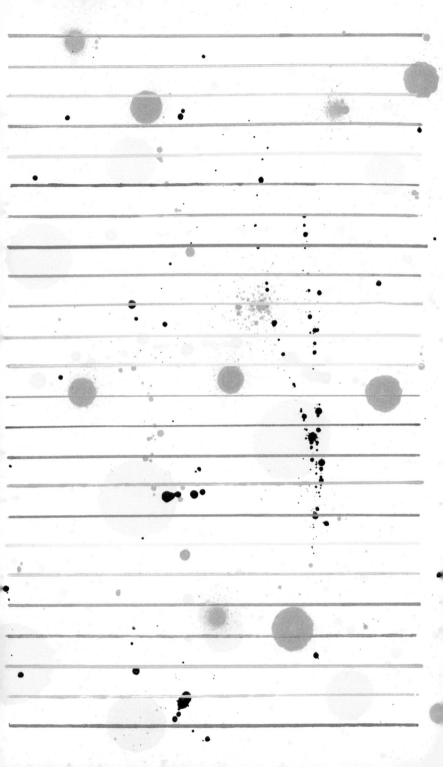

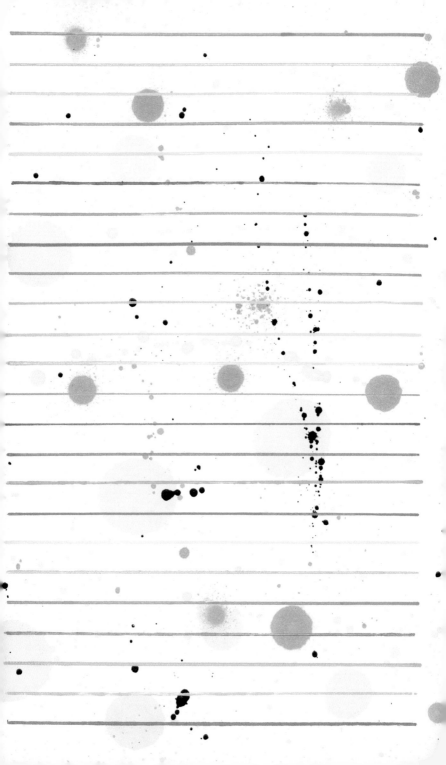

YOU
ALONE
ARE ENOUGH.
YOU HAVE *nothing*
TO **Prove**
TO ANYBODY.

-maya angelou

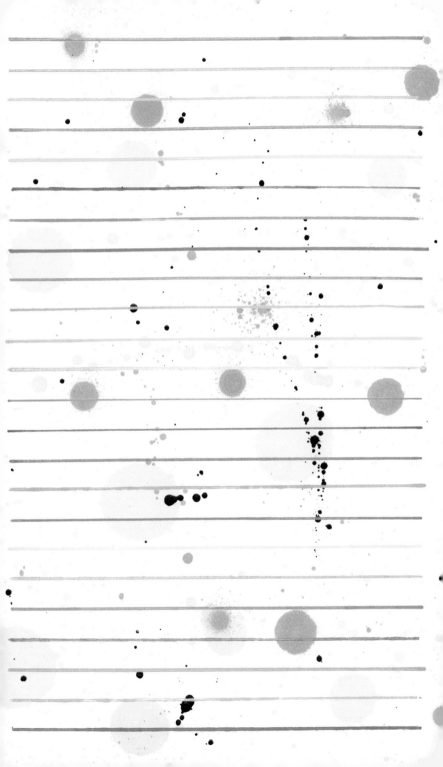

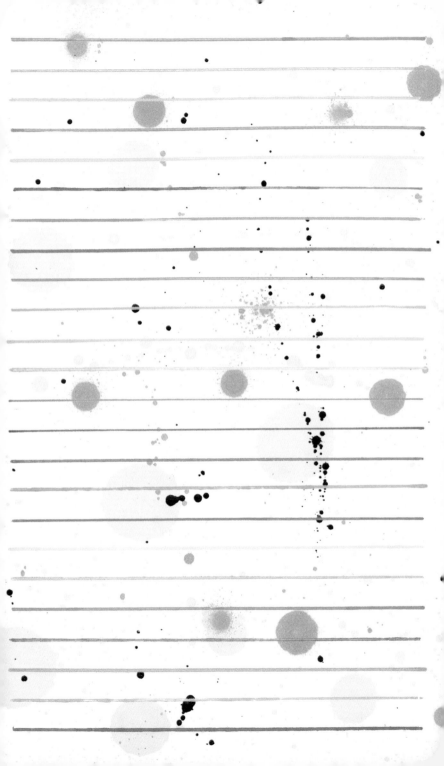

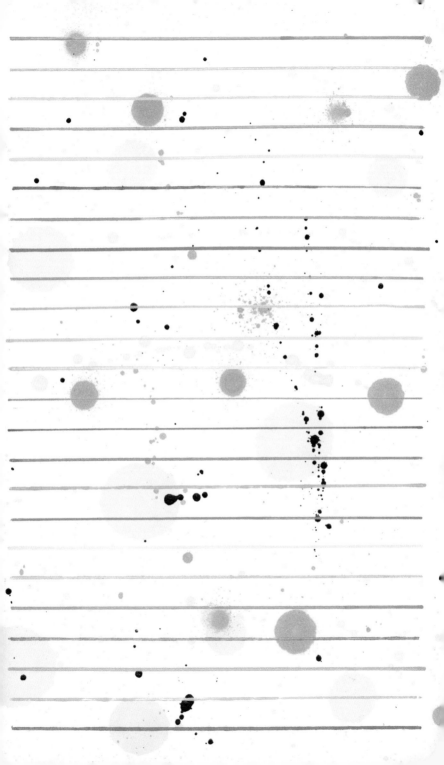

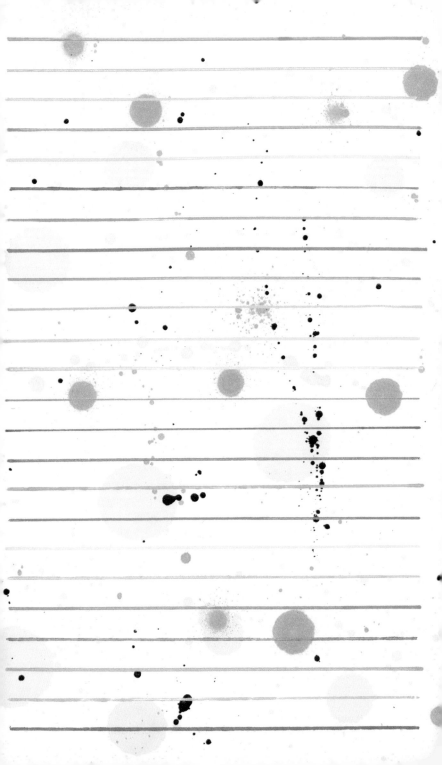

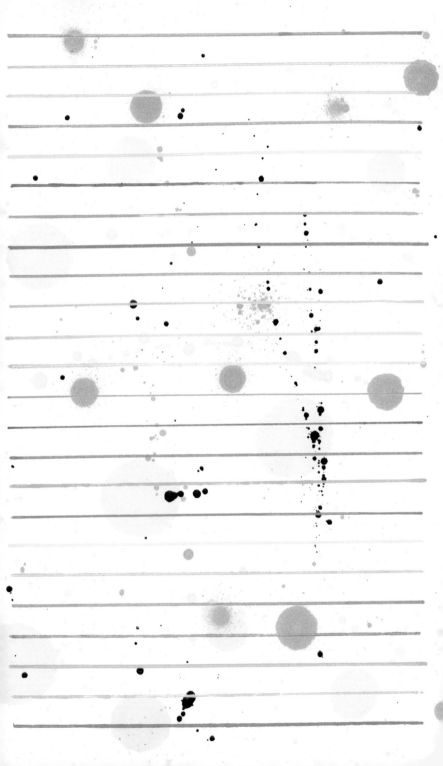

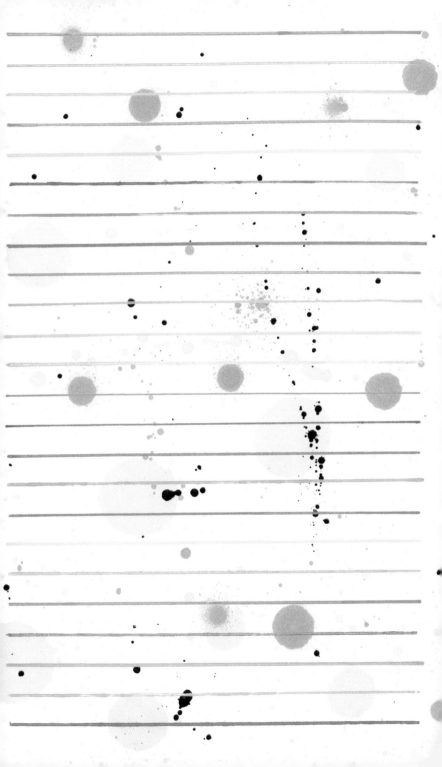

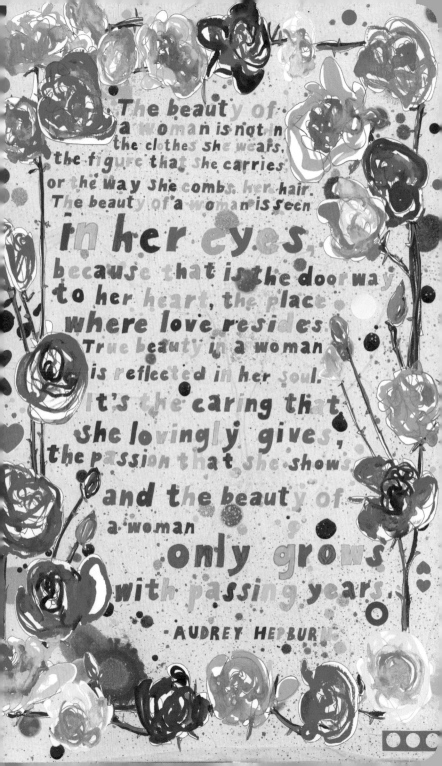

The beauty of a woman is not in the clothes she wears, the figure that she carries or the way she combs her hair. The beauty of a woman is seen **in her eyes,** because that is the doorway to her heart, the place where love resides. True beauty in a woman is reflected in her soul. It's the caring that she lovingly gives, the passion that she shows and the beauty of a woman **only grows** with passing years.

- AUDREY HEPBURN

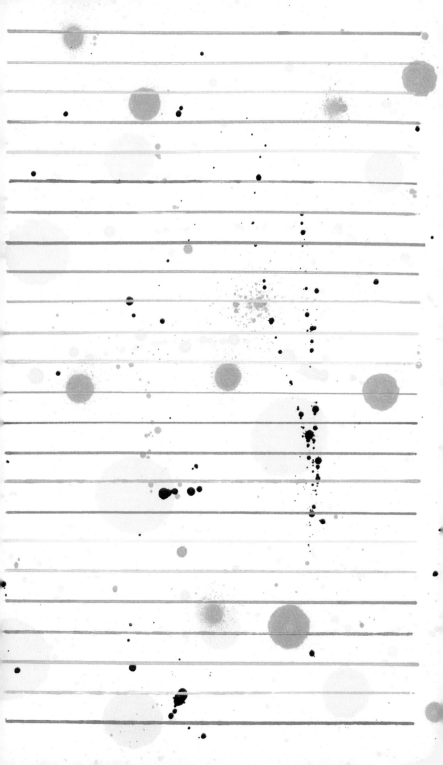

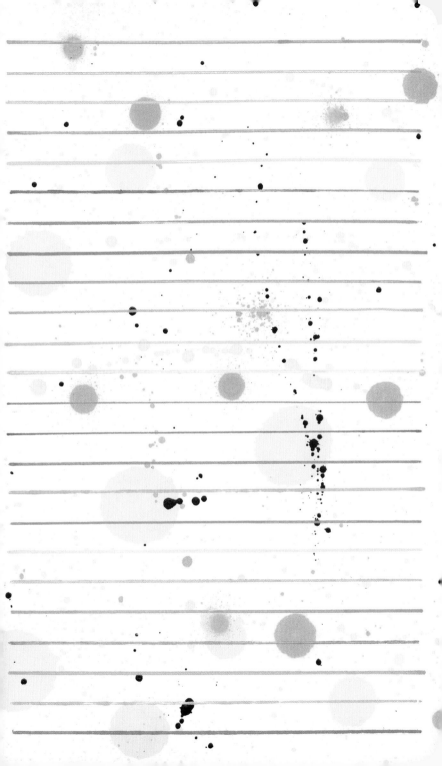

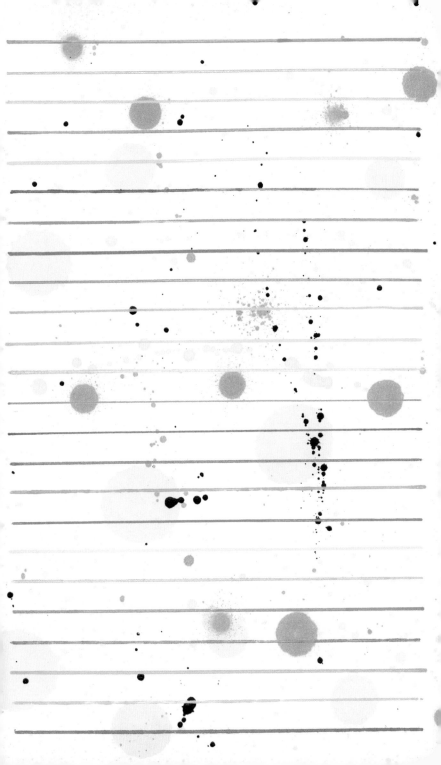

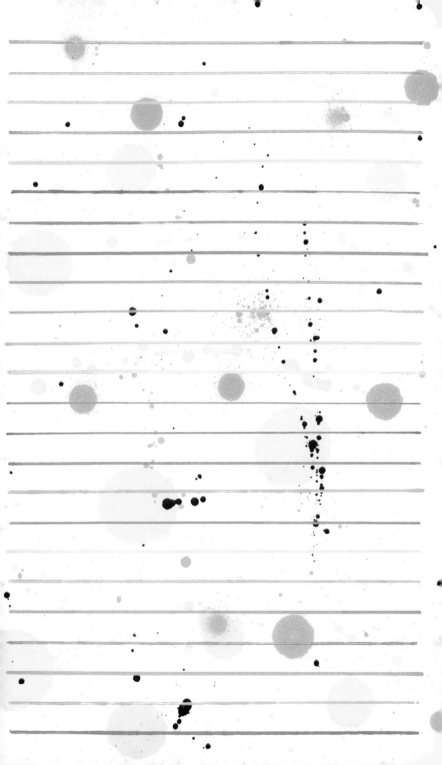

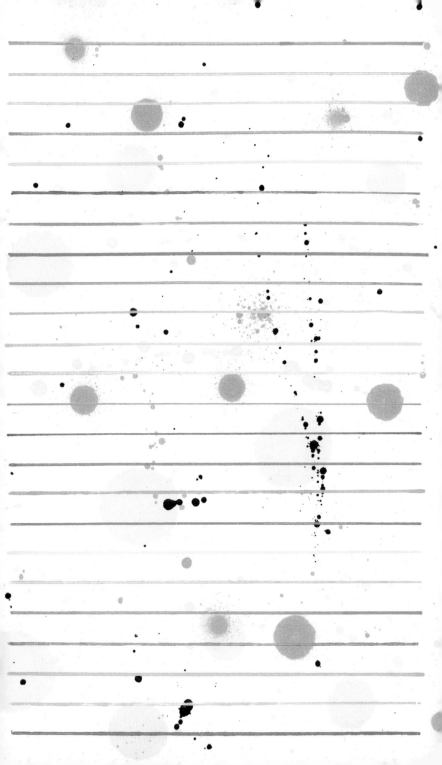

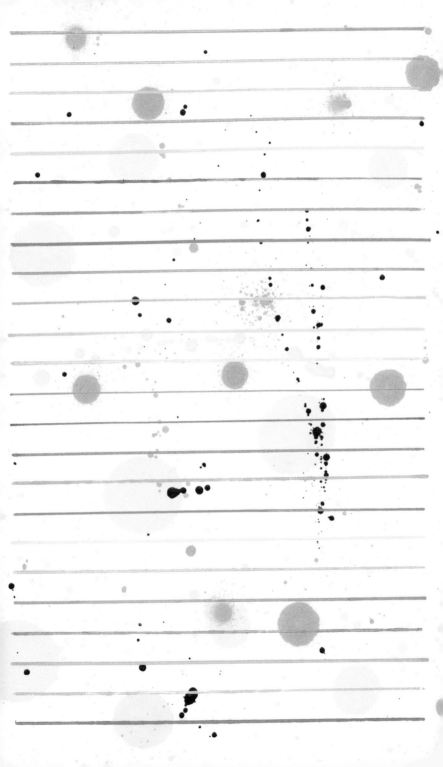

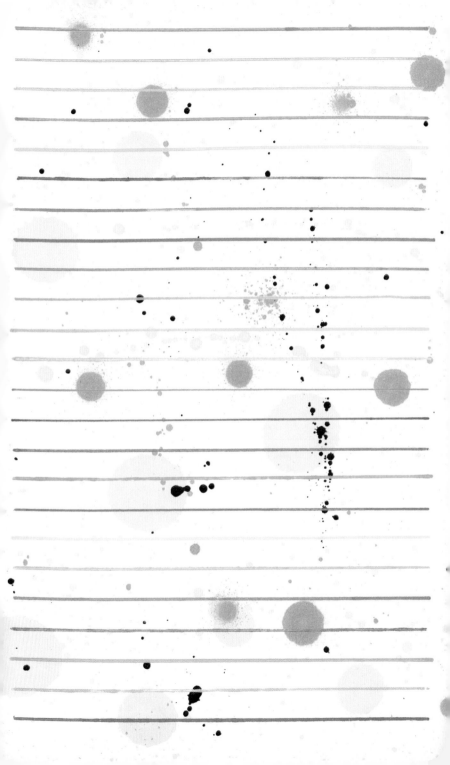